Art in America
By
Aleister Crowley

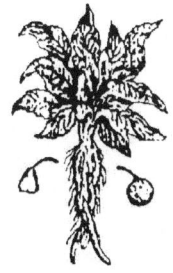

Mandrake chapbook
Imbolc 2024

Preface

Art in America was written for *The English Review* in 1913, this essay perhaps says more about Crowley than American art. It was much criticised by contemporary American artists for its prejudice and unfairness. Crowley says in *The Confessions* that his judgements of past American art was severe, but that he had planned other, more positive essays dealing with the present and its future. The essays lasting value is largely historical, how differently things have come to look in the intervening one hundred years.

Art in America

By Aleister Crowley

Nay, start not at the word! America."
Shelly.

History offers no parallel with the situation of art in America. In the very flower-tide of English literature out go the Pilgrim Fathers with the Bible, Shakespeare, Milton and John Bunyan, into a country whose natural beauties and whose natural vigours seem as if they would force art from the various savages. The history of American development, one might hastily assert, offers every inducement to art in every form.

And yet the result is relative sterility. If we except Poe and Whitman in literature, Whistler and Sargent in painting, these remarks on Art in America seem likely to be as few as those as on Snakes in Ireland.

Do we find anything that even aspires to be the first rank? Poe is not in any sense a local bard: he is of course, universal; yet he seems almost anti-local; most of his stories are drawn from the Old World, or might just as well have happened there. Whistler and Sargent never worked in America at all. The astounding inspiration of much of American scenery, ranging from the cliffs of Yosemite and Niagara to the plains of Texas and the Mississippi, fails to inspire the native. I have at my tongue's tip a dozen superb nature-pictures of their country – God's country! no boasting that! – and every one of them was written by an Irishman or a Scot.

Why could not Whistler had painted in the Yellowstone? The nearest he ever got to it was Valparaiso.

I think the truth of the matter lies in this, that where life is so abundant only the eldest souls can ever begin to turn themselves to that quintessentialising of it which is the secret of art, and that such souls, overwhelmed by its immensity, or lacking in the youth of genius, have failed.

Even of those whom we may claim as at least

candidates for election to the Elysian fields, we must remark that their output is infinitesimal. In prose, it is true, Poe managed to sustain himself in ether well enough, and **The Narrative of Arthur Gordon Pym (**too little known here) is a great achievement than any of the shorter stories. But you can pack away his poetry into a hat-box. "The Raven" is, to my mind, a much over-rated piece; "The Bells" is as bad as Southey's. "How the water comes down at Lodore." What remains? "Ulalume", "Annabelle Lee," "Al Araaf " (more or less), "Israfel" and three or four pieces which are barely more than stanzas.

All very exquisite, all lacking body, and all monotones in a single key.

I say this, although I consider Poe to have been one of the greatest men of his century. The thought in "Eureka", "Monos and Una", and one or two other essays, is profound and lofty. But there is little breath in the depths. His philosophy is based not on a study of all human thoughts, but on odd books which drifted his way. He tried to make bricks without straw, and it was bad for his pyramid.

His book-learning too, slight as it was, was too much valued. He always hinted at his own scholarship. He was "cultured", though with enough real genius to laugh at the "frog-pond" of cultured Boston.

Of American culture, I have one perfect sample. Travelling from Nagasaki to Hong Kong to mature maidens from Massachusetts discovered that I sometimes wrote, and "took me up". "And who", I asked, "is your favourite poet?"

A warm flush overspread each sallow cheek as the two thin mouths exclaimed "Rossetti!" "And which" (I tactlessly pursued) "which of his poems do you like the best?"

This remark closed the conversation. They had put the name Rossetti down in a notebook; and right there "culture" ended.

This I found characteristic of many American women. I have seen American girls in Italy laboriously writing down the names of more painters than I shall ever know, without any further comment than the dates at which they painted. To ask a single question on the broadest lines was to court silence; in fact, it became the most useful method in my daily life and conversation.

The National American Game is poker; and as "calling" in artistic Jackpots, cost nothing, it is a safe rule never to lay down your hand.

It is the same with children. I once talked with a boy of thirteen years old, as bright and intelligence as I ever met. He knew no Latin or any modern language; he did not know where Berlin was; he knew the names of only eight states in his own country, although he was getting "a quarter" for every one he could name; he knew no arithmetic beyond the first four rules, and those he knew badly; his story was confined to George Washington and James G Blaine, to the exclusion of such insignificant characters as Napoleon; and his other mental bunkers were equally empty of coal. He had excellent machinery; nothing for it to work with.

Now, one might expect a boy of this type – a type almost universal in America – to develop into an artist. He lived in Salt Lake City, but spent most of his year in California and Honolulu. Having nothing else to feed on, one would expect him to feed on his surroundings; and I cannot conceive of anything more sublime. The Mormon adventure is one of the most romantic in the world's history; the ghastly grandeur of Utah is an epitome of death as Oahu and the Golden Gate are of life. The finest island in the world; the third finest harbour in the world; the most wonderful valley in the world; and the most admirable climate in the world; one of the most intoxicatingly varied populations in the world - what comes of it?

What do we know of the whole splendour of the people and the place? Just exactly what Robert Louis Stevenson has to tell us: "only that and nothing more!" (Lloyd Osborne, however, is responsible for much of the best of my favourite novel *The Wrecker*.)

This brings me back with a jerk to Edgar Allan Poe. He lives in a land whose every breath is lyric exultation, and the only nature-poetry gives us concerns Venice (in the "assignation") and "the dark lake of Auber in the ghoul-haunted woodland of Weir", which is no more American than Battersea Bridge. The only other picture that rises to my mind is "The House of Usher", which sounds more like Germany or Norfolk.

Whitman is almost equally unconvincing as far as scenery goes. The secret of all Nature-poetry is *the interpretation of every phenomenon as a direct dealing of God with the soul,* and Whitman rarely reaches to be more than a recorder or reflector of Nature. It stirs him at times to big thoughts, but hardly ever in that intimate manner, that sense of necessity, which we see in Keats, Coleridge, and even Wordsworth.

And yet he does something better than all this. He gets it as none other ever got it, the sense of vast open space and the vigorous autochthon rejoicing in his strengths-man made one with the big biggest kind of Nature.

Most of Poe's best scenery is pure imagination; for example, the matter of the

Ice-lands in *Arthur Gordon Pym*; of the realists Mark Twain is the only one worth a moment's consideration. The Mississippi really seems to have impressed him; but it is only in rare moods, and these poetic moods are by no means his best. I find it difficult to refrain from shouting for joy at the immensity of those swirling waters. I understand Beethoven roaring at the sunrise. But Mark Twain at his best is a profaner of those sublimities; the shallow criticism is usually uppermost in his mind. Indeed, one wonders whether there is deeper passages were not written just to show us that he could do it. Was the obvious result that he shows us that he couldn't.

In fact, if we are to take the loftiness of the habitual plane of thought to be the first qualification of a great artist, Poe and Whitman stand alone.

Of these Poe, philosophy and all, is little more than "Thoughts on death", a limitation as bad as that of Degas or Gustav Moreau. There is more deep and more varied thought in a single sonnet of Baudelaire. Poe lives principally by the vividness of his imagery and the excellence of his style. But Europe, in the same century, can name in literature alone fifty artists with superior vision and equal execution.

As to Whitman, I confess that I praise him with an exceeding bad grace. I am cursed with a public school and university education, though luckily I was born with enough native sense to shirk the soulless ritual of its so far as might be, and its bad influence has been corrected by years of wandering in the wilds. How the "scholar" can pretend to admire Whitman one can only explain by theories highly discreditable to the scholar. But, however we may despise the scholar, there are yet natural laws of rhythm. I do not argue that we know them all; on the contrary, I expect every new artist to declare new laws, but I deny that Whitman did so.

As an artist, he appears to me incomparably deficient. There is not one line whose music is retained by memory; I simply fail to understand the people who talk of his "subtle rhythm". I am deaf to it. And though his thought is so finely pantheistic, now and again, what point is there in the quotation from the catalogue of the Army and the Navy Stores, which make up three-quarters of his work? A great mind, perhaps; it seems to me as if that mind has been overwhelmed by the immensity of its material. He obtained such mystic rapture from every object that he could do nothing but scribbled down its name! He has been most praise, too, and has probably achieved much fame, by the perfectly gratuitous coarseness of his phrase whenever that phrase becomes articulate.

It is rather like Satan rebuking sin; but I think that the passage in *A Woman Waits for Me* ending with the words "accumulated within me" is revolting and beastly.

Quite right, someone will say, that pure beastliness should find its expression; the point of view is as well worth recording as any other. Whitman has no doubt expressed the gross animal instinct which growls in man, and I think no man before Whitman ever consciously expressed it to himself. But is it art? Is there any merit in the expression? Is there melody, of fitness of any kind, in it? Why is this more poetic than the remarks expressed in even simpler (and therefore

better) language on the walls of our
"Vespasiennes." (Pissoirs)

What said Blake? "Everything that lives his holy";
"the lust of the goat is the Glory of God"; – true
as truth is self.

But "truth is beauty", too; and the truth of life is
not beautiful like the truth of art, because Art
selects the beautiful like the truth of art, because
Art selects the essential truth, the truth that is
common to all, the "thing-in-itself", and declares
that truth in fitting language. Whitman's language
is occasionally not fitting; it is filthy; it has no
link with eternal truth such as is given by beauty
of expression, by style, which manifests the
internal harmony of the universe.

We should not tolerate such language even in a
newspaper, even in a modern drawing room
whose conversation is confined to enlighten
comment upon works of Professor Von Krafft-
Ebing; but we must praise it, must we, "because
Whitman saw the great vision of the Universal
Unity"? Every artist sees this vision; every truly
religious person sees this vision; many of them

have deemed it most fitting to express this vision by symbolising it as Sex; but not one has made the indecent gesture. In India, many millions worship the Shiva Lingam; it is represented over and over again, in every temple in every material and every size; but there is never anything to shock or disgust. It is not a question of morality – Whitman's morals are in all respects, admirably clean – but of decency; and Whitman's indecencies - I have not quoted the worst - seemed to me as pointless and inane as those of a crew of drunken sailors in a lime house bar. Even in the cleaner poems, the "Song of Myself", the "Song of the Open Road", one gets this conviction of domination of mind by matter which is to me the supreme horror. That and the monstrous egoism of the man, the bombast and crudity alike of thought and utterance, leave me with a feeling that I did well indeed to close my Whitman, after a conscientious perusal, never to open it again, at least with the idea of attaining anything of worth.

I think that the real ground of his reputation lies in the very uncouthness of his form, and in the fact that once said: "Here is an American voice in tune with the most advanced voices of Europe." Max Nordau, too, in classing him with the great men whom his spite prompted him to spit upon from an altitude of about million miles beneath their boots, gave him an altogether false importance.

In Art a man's views count for nothing. It is a curious paradox that a man can only write if he is so white-hot over something that his work pours through him, not from him; and yet, it is not of the least importance what that something is.

I agree with Walter Pater; but I know that Bunion, with whom I disagree, was first-rate, and Pater second-rate.

What does it matter with anyone *is* right? If he *does* tight, it will last.

This tirade is, however, to be taken as from the point of view of the purely literary mind. It is easy enough for the university-trained European to avoid blenders, which shock purists in. Walt Whitman, and we consequently obtain a quite a quite false idea that such European work is "good."

From the philosophical, and even more from the humane view, Whitman is an artist supreme in so far as he mirrors the spirit of his time and country. He has the childish petulance and bombast and enthusiasm, the gross, naked lust and the ultra-refined delicacy, the essential rough vigour, the hurry, the conceit, the egoism, the astounding incompetence and the still more astounding capacity, the jingoism, even the cant of the American-as-he-is-in-himself, the Yank *an sich*. I find me meaning even in the strings of names; I understand how, in a country so new and generous, the mere crying of the names of things fills the soul with ecstasy - the ecstasy of poetry. Whitman, says "lint", bandages, iodoform" as the Greeks said "Thalassa! Thalassa!" (*The Sea! The Sea!* All language is hieroglyphic, from the blessed word Mesopotamia downwards. When I was a child my favourite Bible readings were the genealogies with the far-sounding names.) And thereby conjures a vision of all the heroism and suffering of the War of Succession. That war was never sung, as we understand song. But there is

many a heart a thrill at "O tan-faced prairie boy."
Two "lines" which are not lines! Yet the
superhuman rapture of an unexpected love in the
open air - not beyond experience, I hope, those
who live there! - Is given, naked and gorgeous
beyond all royal pomp, in those two lines that are
not lines.

All this America is crude, formless, hurried,
crowded. There is little real music, even of the
simpler lyrics sort, in the Americans. "Culture" is
a pose; even common education sits ill on him.
We must not expect his literature to follow our
lines. His literature is to come. We shall know
when it does - it will be stupendous, it will be
gigantic and elemental beyond all experience. It
will keep our rules. It can only come with a
settlement of some of the main social and
political problems; but when it does, we shall, I
believe, clearly recognize Walt Whitman as the
fountain and origin of all.

I am well aware that I am thus placing on the
highest of all possible pinnacles a man whom I
detest and despise; but I deliberately do so. A

Balaam (*Bible*, Numbers 22 to 24.) come to Judgment!

Whitman is America. Here's the real thing, the spirit of the new continent made word. Not the voice of imported culture, or of anything inessential. He is raw, untutored, tame less, crude, the America of the War. I have lived on the prairie myself, and I recognized the note.

The claim of Emerson, Longfellow, Bryant, Whittier and the rests are more easily dealt with. Emerson's ruggedness saves him from the barber's assistant fate of the others. In some ways Emerson is quite the greatest of the Americans. His outlook is wide, and his thought profound; but his speech (as far as the poetry is concerned) is very imperfect, and (as far as the prose is concerned) too perfect, while the quantity of his best work is quite negligible if we think of Carlyle or Nietzsche. Nor do the essays rank with Bacon or Montaigne.

Longfellow is merely the polite professor; he has little learning, even for an undergraduate, and he has never penetrated a single mu into the varnish of any drawing room idea. Smooth, shallow optimism, as faith even more frock-coated and silk-hatted than Tennyson's, a style absolutely wooden.

Said Poe, having printed a long passage of "Evangeline" as prose: "There is good respectable prose, and no one will ever again run the danger of mistaking it for poetry." There are one or two lyrics, good second-class, for example:

"The day is done, and the darkness

Falls and the wings of night

As a feather is wafted downward

From an eagle in its flight."

This is fairly fine poetry. It is simple; the image is clear and coherent, as well as beautiful; and the infinite purpose of the universe is suggested by the introduction of the eagle. But there is not much else of this calibre; most of Longfellow is popgun loaded with popcorn. Bryant is, on the whole, even more spectacle than Longfellow; and

Whittier is little better than Moody and Sankey. (Nineteenth century American evangelists.)

If most of these people have lived in England, should we have a quarter as much fuss made about them? But in the desert which Childe Roland crossed "a burr, had been a treasure-trove."

Of Bryant the best quotation which Poe (who was trying to extol him) can find are this sort of thing:

"And what if cheerful shouts at noon
Come, from the village sent,
Or songs of maids beneath the moon
With fairy laughter blent?
And what if, in the evening light,
Betrothed lovers walked in sight
Of my low monument?"
Echo answers "what?" A sonnet beginning
"Ay, thou art for the grave,"

ends

"We will trust in God to see thee yet again."

After this we wander if Poe was not smiling softly to himself in concluding his appreciation: "He is married (Mrs Bryant still living), has two daughters (one of them Mrs Parke Godwin), and is residing for the present at Vice-Chancellor McCown's, near the junction of Warren and Church streets."

Walter Savage Landor was an exile in Italy, and in any case I find it difficult to read him. How he came to conquer Swinburne one cannot imagine, unless one knows all about Swinburne.

Nathaniel Hawthorne and Washington Irving are difficult to rank in the first class. The sentimentality of the one and the obviousness of the other are enough to bar them from the Immortals. And Hawthorne at least was caught red handed in a very open plagiary. In their time and place, however, they stood for a good deal of good. They did excellent work of its kind. **R.I.P**.

Of others who had their measure of fame some seventy years ago, there are some surprisingly facile writers.

Amelia Welby had these excellent lines. I cannot quote better from any English writer:

"And softly through the forest bars
Light lovely shapes, on glossy plumes,
Float even in, like winged stars,
Amid the purpling glooms."

And keeps it up more or less when nearly fifty lines.

But this is very solitary swallow.

May I be pardoned a note of flippancy in dealing with the rank and file?

Their names are forgotten even by their umquhile flatterers. I revive them because one or two of them, were most richly endowed by Mr. Robert Ross' favourite 10th Muse – the "Muse of Bad Poetry."

Seba Smiths, for instance, became immortal on this:

"But bravely to the river's brink

I led my warrior train,

And face to face each glance they sent

We sent it back again.

Their werowance looked stern at me,

And I look stern at him."

Of the Channings, one need only remark that the uncle was a pedant and the nephew an ignoramus.

Kentucky, however, produced a very fine few lines from the pen of Mr. William Wallace:

He saw:

"A swathe of purple, gold and amethyst

And luminous, behind the billowing mist

Something that looked to my young eyes like God."

Of course, one might object to mixing purple and amethyst; but the last two lines are first class.

Only-only-only – there it seems to stop. He never wrote anything else.

Anna Lewis talks about "Rapine and Vice" disporting "on Glory's gilded tomb" and "the dark inscrutable decrees of Fate," and we pass rapidly to the Reverend Joel T Headley, who wrote the most comic account of the Crucifixion that has ever been penned. It is impossible to transcribe it, unless in a professedly religious journal, without risking the ire of Mr. Joseph McCabe and the other supporters of the Laws against Blasphemy.

George P Morris, of whom I know little but that he is dead, appears to have been the original of Frederick E Weatherly and Mr. Clifford Clifton Bingham.

There seems also to have been a Robert M Bird, who would have imitated Sir Walter Scott well enough if his mind had not so constantly wandered.

And there was undoubtedly one Cornelius Matthews, who burst his poetic gun the very first time he fired it.

W G Simms was at one time exceedingly popular as a writer of short stories; they resemble those of Poe, but lack alike his genius and his style. Still, they are good enough to alarm the older writer, and perhaps it is a pity that they are now only to be found in the national collections. Ambrose Bierce has at least one magnificent short story to his credit.

James Russell Lowell is better known in England than any of the last dozen I have mentioned; but his work is altogether without merit. It is the worst journalese, and the man was hardly better than a political hack. His success is worth no more than that of a new kind of pole-cat might be.

The only touch of true satire that I recall is the excellent

"I dew believe in freedom's cause.

As fur away as Paris is."

Henry James, good or bad, is too important and too *sub judice* to say to discuss in this brief appreciation of the literary stars that spangle Old Glory.

Another writer well known in England is Fennimore Cooper. He, again succeeded chiefly by the novelty of his themes; his method is stilted, and after all, he is only boyhood's friend. That I still like him only proves – what everybody knows – that I have never grown up.

But I do like him, and, if pressed, will maintain against a world that his pictures of the manners of an extinct race may be one day the most trustworthy data that posterity can command. (But what has that to do with Art?)

There are some dozens of others, Sprague, Dana, Hulleck, Willis, Hoyt, Hunt, Anthon Bush, Cheever, Mowatt, Francis, English, Stephens, Cranch, Dyckink, Aldrick, Krikland, Fuller, Epes. W W Lord, Sedgwick, Clark, Walsh, Child, Hewitt Hoffman, Ward, Richard Adams Locke, Wilmer, Kettell. Brainard, Hirst, Drake and the prince of them all, Rufus Dewes, author of Geraldine with its immortal climax. He lay gentle down. Bereft and sank his picture on her bosoms snow. Post behind these lines in blood, he left. Farewell forever, "Geraldine" with its immortal climax:

"He laid gentle down, of sense bereft,
And sank his picture on her bosom's snow
And close beside these lines in blood he left:
Farewell forever, Geraldine, I go
Another woman's victim – dare I tell?
'Tis Alice – curse us, Geraldine! Farewell!

Of all these there is not one whose name is today familiar to any American of whom I have inquired, though W W Lord made a big bid for fame – of a sort – by his impudence in publishing.

"And the aged beldames napping,
Dreamed of gently rapping, rapping,
With a hammer gently tapping,
Tapping on an infant's skull."
Ward is best known by his
"Bees buzzed and wrens that thronged the rushes
Poured round incessant twittering gushes."

and the inimitable

"Oh, curl in smiles that mouth again,
And wipe that weeper dry!"

I momentarily forget – the world will remember – who wrote:

"His sinuous path, by blazes, wound
Amongst trunks grouped in myriads round."

But it matters nothing. The conclusion of the whole matter is that English is rare – one gets constantly "done" for "did", "took" for "taken," and the like – music rarer still; imagery and thought alike, almost never stirring from the commonplace unless to fall into the abyss of the absurd.

I have not exhausted the list of claimants to literary fame; but Mark Twain's "James Ragsdale McClintock," whoever he was, is not really very much worse than the rest.

I have a prize specimen of my own, but (for all I know) he is still living, while this article is principally concerned with the dead, and, besides, I have endeavoured elsewhere to divert the discerning public very greatly with him in an article entirely devoted to so rare a bird.

We can then fold our wings sadly over our faces, when we contemplate the past (in this article I avoid dealing with the present) of American literature.

It must, however, be remembered that it dates back very few years indeed. There are no American contemporaries of even Shelly. Why should there have been? They were too busy as pioneers. The only bright spot is the humour; and of course humour is the most perishable of all commodities. American humour, especially, depends almost entirely on local realism, and the railway changes that.

When we turned to Art, it is even bleaker prospect. After Whistler and Sargant, the former not even really an American, and both exiles from America by adoption, there is literally nobody at all 'till we strike the geological stratum of Penrhyn Stanlaws (whose name is Adamson, and whose birthplace Dundee!) and Charles Dana Gibson, of whose parentage one neither knows nor wishes to know anything.

One may reproach me with a forgetting Alexander Harrison, who once painted two quite passable pictures, by accident, at the age of 32 to 33, "The

Wave" and "In Arcady". The former of these is actually the first purely marine picture ever painted, and one may consequently class the artist with the immortals for historical importance. But of course he has always lived and worked in France, and he has never added a third passable picture to the former two.

Turn to music: I do not know of anything, except McDowell's work, which even pretends to be ambitious or to have any real connection with anything beyond musical comedy and dollars.

The only American sculptor that I know of is a Lithuanian living in Paris. (Presumably Jacob Epstein, born New York in 1880.)

No American actress has made any mark on serious acting, but that question is beside the point. Nearly all actors are Jews, in America as elsewhere. Only one really great singer has hailed from Colombia, and one incomparable dancer, I speak of Jenny Lind and Isadora Duncan.

Even the national hymn. "My country, 'tis of thee," is little better than a parody of "God save the king": And I have heard the Imperial Japanese band at the state festival perform "After the Ball", under the impression that it was the national anthem of their guests of the evening.

It may be remarked in passing, that America only produced one really great man of science – Simon Newcomb (1835 to 1909) Astronomer. The boasted inventions of the Americans do not exist. What they invent is "notions" based on the discovery of others. Edison is merely an organizer and adapter of scientific brains; the telephone itself was due to Bell, an Englishman. I cannot think of anyone scientific discovery of the first importance, which was made in the United States. In Europe we have Kelvin, Helmholtz, Hertz, Haeckel, Darwin, Young, Lister, Pasteur – the pen runs on, one could fill a page from memory. I studied chemistry, physics and biology pretty thoroughly at one time: I do not recall any American name in the textbooks. Such men, as we know, are like Tesla and Lowell, who are not even serious. We must absolve America from Tesla, however, as he is but a recently imported product. In medicine the only name that occurs is Weir Mitchell, and all that he did was to point out that overworked people had better stay in bed. Of course, there is an enormous amount of work of second rate importance, but none as the first rank.

As in philosophy, we have even less material for our criticism. The earliest figure in American philosophical literature of any notoriety is George Starkey, the Alchemist, there is, however, nothing very distinctive about him. It needs an expert to tell him from Fludd Ripley or Sendivogius.

After him, no name awakes in memory until Emerson, and Emerson did nothing particularly new. William James is the only name occurs to me with anything like a feeling of respect. (The feeling is, however, very strong: I think the "Varieties of religious experience" one of the most important books ever published. But why did the good man waste such a lot of time on Mrs Piper? Automatic writing will never open the gates of immortality.)

A sorry story!

And why is it? Why is that, that with everything

in favour of new birth, of "variation", we find so very little born? Consider the astounding avidity with which the Americans swallow every kind of idea, the rage for literature, the subsidizing of Art, the passion for music. Consider even the new blood that pours into the States to the tune of two millions a year from every art producing country in Europe: and wonder grows, and grows.

Americans say that the immigrants are the scum of Europe. Perhaps, but they beat the native out of most of his money and power in no time. Isn't there a touching song about the "poor exile of Erin" who in a fortnight became "Alderman Mike inthrojuicing a bill"?

There is, firstly, the question of all critical faculty. This is a curiously infantine in nearly all Americans. A man will determine to study philosophy. To whom does he go? To Kant? To Hume? To Aristotle? Dear me, no! He is quite happy with Fra Elbertus, with his sham Kelmscott press (Elbert Hubbard and Roycroft press) and his platitudes, or with Swami Vivekananda, that burliest of Babus. It never strikes him to defer to the Upanishads, from which Vivekananda derived all that is of value in his work.

He is satisfied with any good machine made stuff; he really thinks that Swinburne was "the English Ella Wheeler Wilcox." When it comes to criticism of "Old Masters," he rarely looks at them with the eyes that God has given him; he looks through the spectacles of a guidebook.

Not that the English are not equally incapable in that respect; but they appear less ignorant, because they are fixed in traditional opinions, which are (on the whole) right. The American cannot stay here; he is restless; he wants to know - and this would ultimately save him - but as yet he has only learned to know *via* Baedeker, and the moment he is off track, he is hopelessly lost.

The Englishman would be as bad, but he knows the danger, and confines himself to the remark that Shakespeare was a great poet. Show him the Futurists, and he holds out a confiding hand to any professional or amateur leg-Puller that may be about.

The "Ministry of all Talents" of Art – Leader,

Marcus Stone, Poynter, Leighton, Sidney Cooper, and so on – do well enough in England; anything like genius is suspect, as Beardsley found. But the American cannot distinguish between Goya and Gerald Kelly; and if he prefers Leader to the others, it is because he remembers "some scandal about a swan." No artist has any advantage with an American; he is perfectly fair, and if he were not also perfectly ignorant, he would make an ideal critic. As a matter of fact, I have sometimes met Americans whose native good sense made them finely appreciative of good work. But they are too often "put off their game" by the comments of "cultured" posers, usually of that Press which has discovered that "women is the market", and thought it best to write down to the assumed level of woman's intellect.

Now, as Wilde urged, criticism is the foundation of creation; at least, it is the negative side of creation. And so, with no power selection from the enormous mass of material at his disposal, he is entirely incompetent to do much more than copy the people he admires. In England we find people imitating Keats, or Swinburne, or Tennyson; in America they can sometimes be found doing their best to produce replicas of Anthony Hope. Note pseudonym or Sir Anthony Hope! (Pseud. of Sir Anthony Hope Hawkins, best remembered for his "Prisoner of Zenda.")

The second point for our consideration is that of climate. I am sometimes tempted to believe that climate is the only thing that matters. Now New York, for example, is in the latitude of Madrid, and can be a great deal hotter than Madrid. The people consequently tend to behave like the Madrilènes. However, the Puritan conscience is in absolute antipathy to the lazily, lazily, drowsily, drowsily frame of mind. So the people "get a move on" and restlessly rage throughout their day - and get nothing done. "Festina lente and "More haste, less speed" ought to be painted up on every street corner in New York.

Of course, the condition of thing does not obtain in every town or in every country.

Toronto makes a Sunday in a Scotcs village seem like a hashish dream!

In short, there is every variety of life and every

variety of scene, and every variety of climate and surroundings.

How is it that every variety is barren? One might not expect a Goethe or a Rodin; there is - outside the cities, where any work is impossible owing to the jolting- a sort of isolation from the pulse of the world, which might (conceivably-though I don't see why it should) inhibit the manifestation of that cosmic sense which is the principal asset of the artist; but at least America might have produced a Herrick or a Burns. The continent is epic in mass, lyric in detail, dramatic in motion, dithyrambic in rest - and nothing comes of it. Is it because no settled order of things, no standard acquiesced in for centuries? Sometimes I think it must be that, Archimedes must have a fulcrum for his lever. In Europe the overturning of the dynasties has usually been the signal for an outburst of every kind of art. Here, however, there is in a sense nothing to overturn. People drift from Methodism to Zionism through Theosophy, Christian Science and Nut-foodism, without a single wavelet over their mental gunwale. If you tell a man that a black is white, he gets thoughtful, and says: "Yes, stranger, I guess that is so."

Nothing is a shock; nothing shatters a great citadel in the soul. Hence no fireworks when the fortress falls, which is does at the blast of no ram's horn, but at the rattling of dried peas in an ass's skull!

If this is not a satisfactory explanation, one must fall back upon the old platitudes about America being a "very *young* country." It is true: there is so much to do that; no one has time to reflect. Poetry is born in the stillness of the soul; boredom is one of its chief stimuli.

The actual life of America is anything but favourable to art production; and there is such exuberance of vitality that there is no need of its concentration. America, too, is a great place for mute inglorious Miltons; a thousand poets might write masterpieces, and we never hear of it. The commercialism of the country is too rampant.

And yet (in conclusion!) the record of America is not bad. Giant inducements, no doubt, but also giant obstacles, and this - deeper and higher than all – that, take one thing with another, man is not equal to his circumstances. Art comes when man has understood his milieu, mastered his life.

There is one poet that has spent most of his life among mountains. He has sung a good deal of the hills of Cumberland, written a little of the Alps, made a poem or so on the mountains of Mexico, an allusion here and there to the Himalayas, though he spent more time in the last than first, and the impression was a thousand fold more intense. The Himalayas are too big for anybody to sing and America is all Himalayas of one kind or another.

No doubt, when immigration stops, when the negro problem, and the Japanese problem, and the labour problem, and the political problem, and all the rest of the problems are solved, when a class arises which has time to reflect upon life instead of living it, American art will lead the world.

Until then, the theme is likely to continue to overwhelm the artist. Whitman alone has risen to the height of destiny; and Whitman was baulked by his own mind.

He was Being without Form as Poe was Form without Being; and creation is the marriage of these twain.

If you enjoyed this book
and want to know more about the author's
other books, many published by Mandrake,
visit our website mandrake.uk.net
where you can also sign up for our free
monthly book newsletter.

A subscription page should pop-up

or type this link into a browser

http://eepurl.com/THE9P

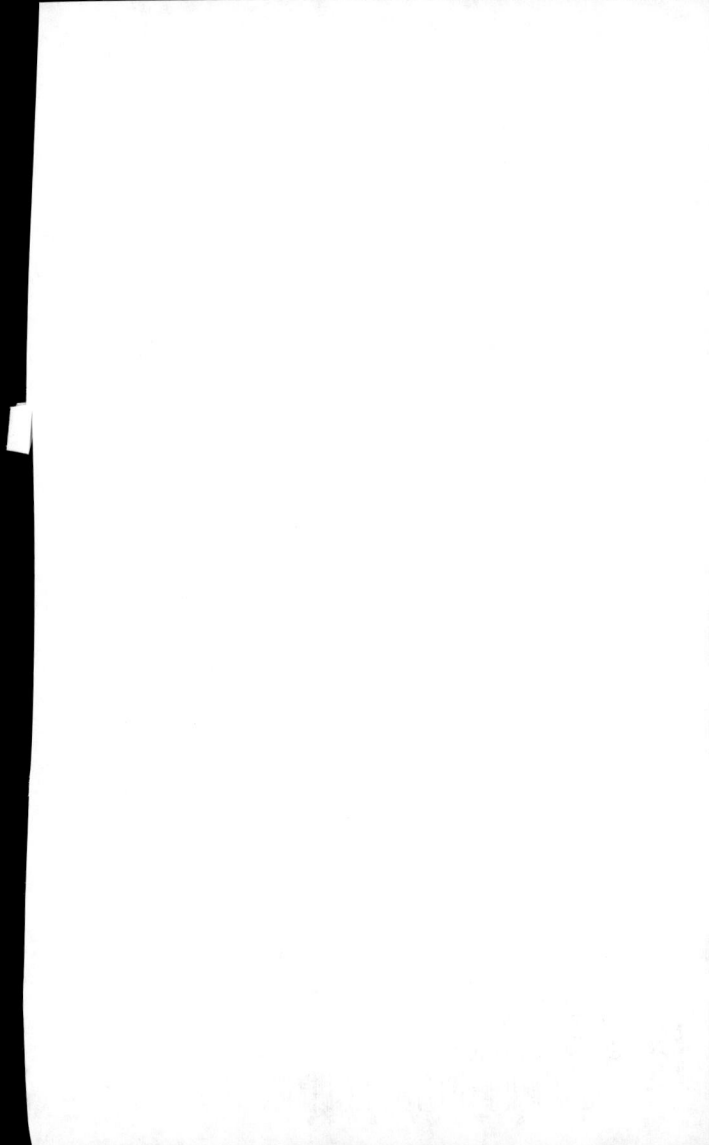